Alfred's Basic Piano Li

Piano

Lesson Book
Level 1B

Correlated materials to be used with *Lesson Book, Level 1B:*

*Teacher's discretion.
**May be used upon completion of Lesson Book 1B, before the student begins Lesson Book 2.

A General MIDI disk (20660) and a Compact Disc (14543) are available, which include a full piano recording and background accompaniment.

Theory Games Software correlating to Levels 1A–5 is available for Macintosh and IBM/Windows-compatible computers.

Willard A. Palmer • Morton Manus • Amanda Vick Lethco

Third Edition
Copyright © MCMXCIX by Alfred Publishing Co., Inc.
All rights reserved. Printed in USA.
ISBN 0-88284-789-9
Illustrations by David Silverman (Painted by Cheryl Hennigar)

Review

THE GRAND STAFF

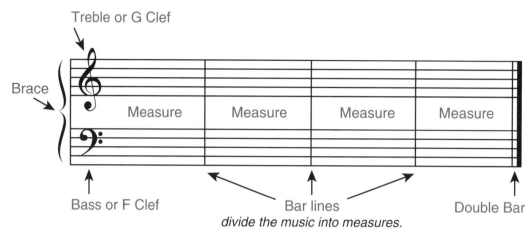

Treble or G Clef

Brace

Measure   Measure   Measure   Measure

Bass or F Clef

Bar lines
divide the music into measures.

Double Bar

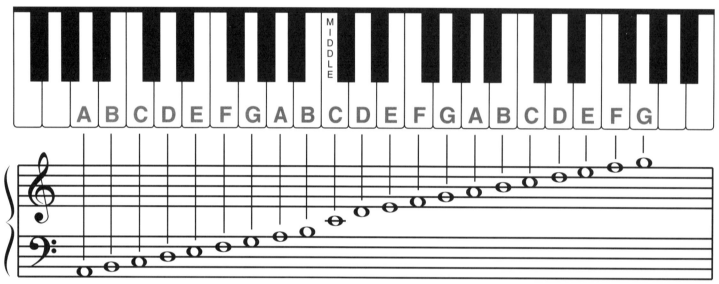

A B C D E F G A B C D E F G A B C D E F G

MIDDLE

TIME SIGNATURE

4 means **4** beats to each measure.
4 a **QUARTER NOTE** ♩ gets one beat.

DYNAMIC SIGNS

tell how LOUD or SOFT to play.

mf (mezzo forte) = moderately loud

NOTE VALUES

♩ = QUARTER NOTE
    Count "1"

♩ = HALF NOTE
    Count "1 - 2"

𝅝 = WHOLE NOTE
    Count "1 - 2 - 3 - 4"

REST VALUES

𝄽 = QUARTER REST
    Count "1"

▬ = HALF REST
    Count "1 - 2"

▬ = WHOLE REST
    Count "1 - 2 - 3 - 4"
    (or rest for a whole measure)

You are now ready to begin THEORY BOOK, Level 1B.

C Position Review

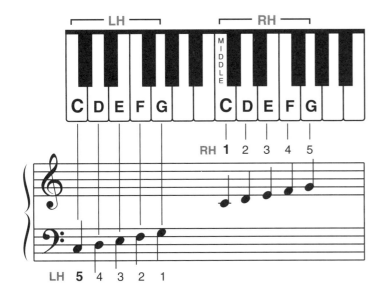

Play and say the note names.

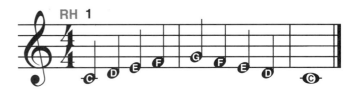

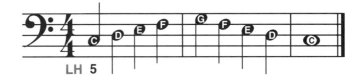

Step Right Up!

1. Clap (or tap) & count.
2. Play & count.
3. Play & sing the words.

Follow these steps for each piece in this book!

Moderately slow

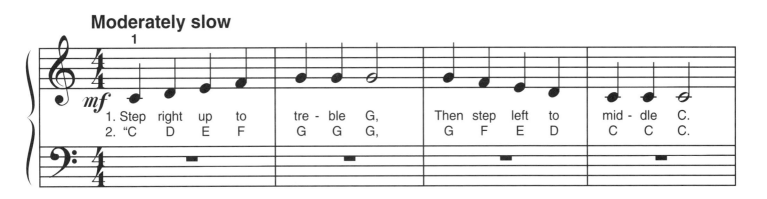

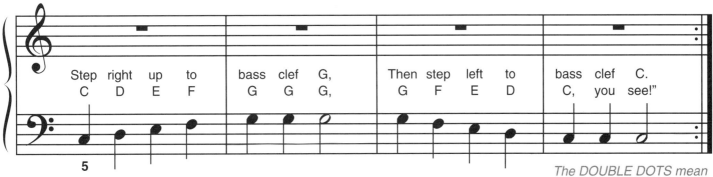

The DOUBLE DOTS mean REPEAT FROM THE BEGINNING.

Review—Melodic Intervals

Distances between tones are measured in **INTERVALS,** called 2nds, 3rds, 4ths, 5ths, etc.

Notes played SEPARATELY make a MELODY.
We call the intervals between these notes **MELODIC INTERVALS.**

Play these MELODIC INTERVALS. Listen to the sound of each interval.

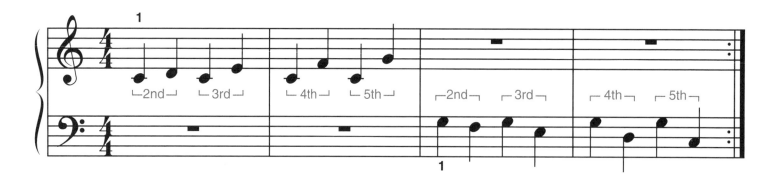

The Carousel

Name all the MELODIC INTERVALS
in this piece before you play it.

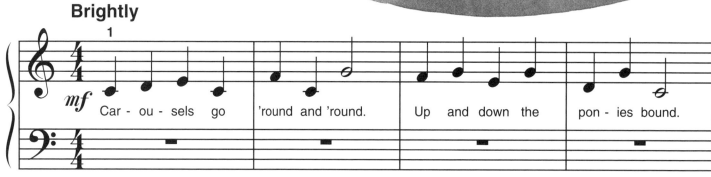

Hail to Thee, America!

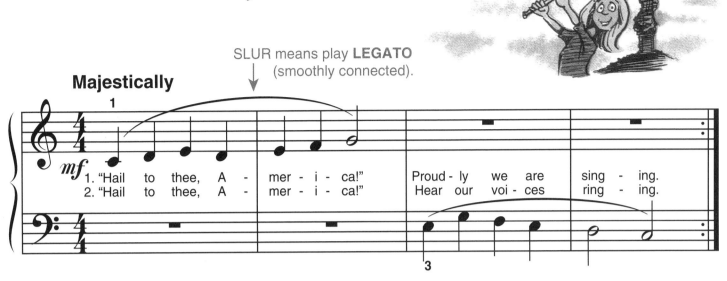

SLUR means play **LEGATO** (smoothly connected).

SLURS often divide the music into phrases (musical thoughts).

p *(piano)* = soft   ***f*** *(forte)* = loud

Brother John

You are now ready to begin TECHNIC BOOK, Level 1B.

Review—Harmonic Intervals

Notes played TOGETHER make HARMONY.
We call the intervals between these notes **HARMONIC INTERVALS.**

Play these HARMONIC INTERVALS. Listen carefully to the sound of each interval.

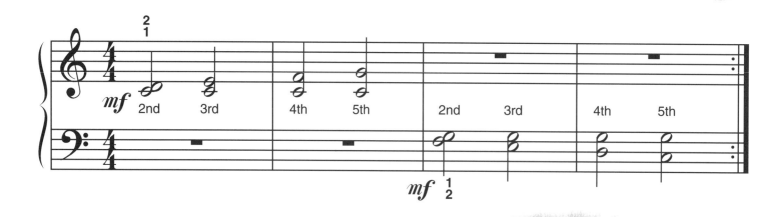

Good Sounds

Moderately fast

You are now ready to begin RECITAL BOOK, Level 1B.

TIME SIGNATURE (Review)

3/4 means **3** beats to each measure.

a **QUARTER NOTE** ♩ gets one beat.

♩. = **DOTTED HALF NOTE**
Count "1 - 2 - 3"

The Cuckoo

First play the left hand alone,
naming each HARMONIC INTERVAL.

Happily

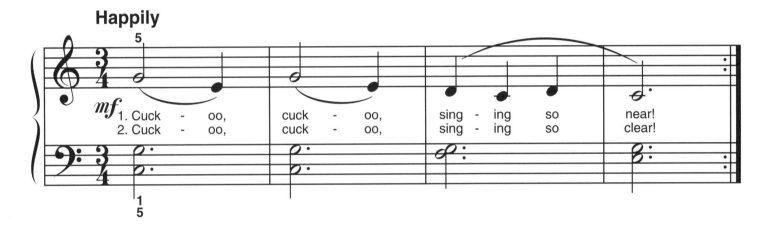

mf
1. Cuck - oo,   cuck - oo,   sing - ing so   near!
2. Cuck - oo,   cuck - oo,   sing - ing so   clear!

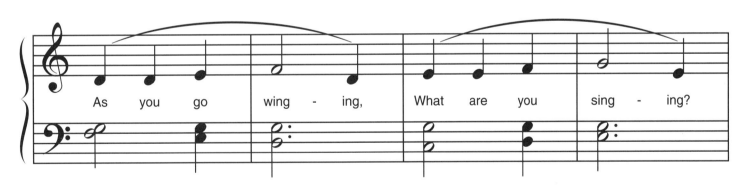

As you go   wing - ing,   What are you   sing - ing?

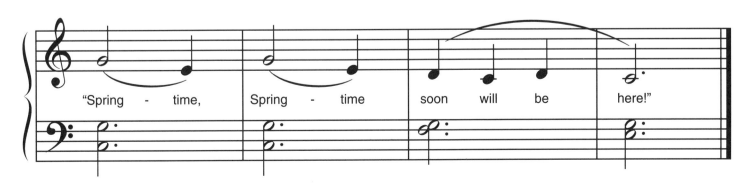

"Spring - time,   Spring - time   soon will be   here!"

You are now ready to begin EAR TRAINING BOOK, Level 1B.

8

Reviewing the SHARP SIGN

 The SHARP SIGN before a note means play the next key to the right, whether BLACK or WHITE.

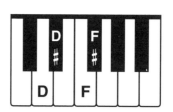

When a SHARP SIGN appears before a note, it applies to that note for the rest of the measure.

Money Can't Buy Ev'rything!

March time

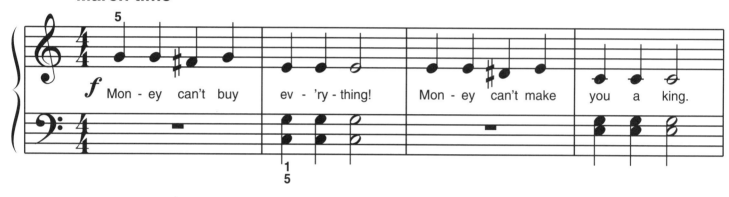

f Mon - ey can't buy   ev - 'ry - thing!   Mon - ey can't make   you   a   king.

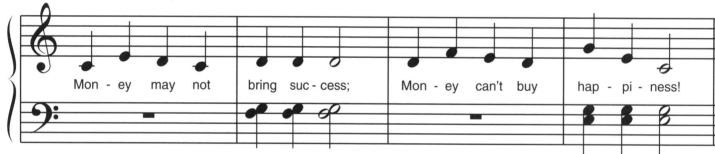

Mon - ey   may   not   bring suc - cess;   Mon - ey can't buy   hap - pi - ness!

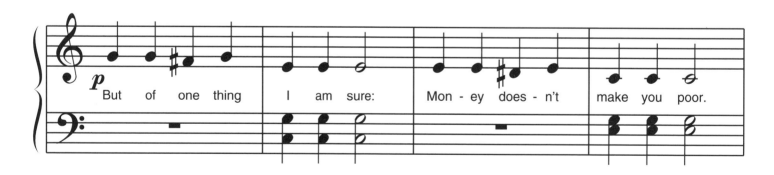

p But   of   one   thing   I   am   sure: Mon - ey does - n't   make   you   poor.

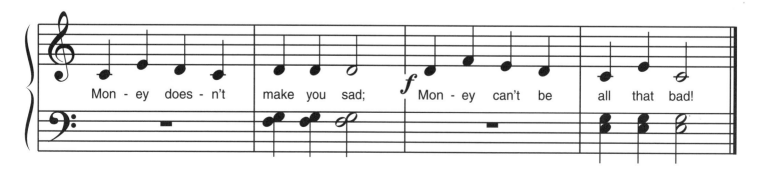

Mon - ey does - n't   make you   sad;   *f* Mon - ey   can't   be   all   that   bad!

STACCATO (Review)

STACCATO is the opposite of LEGATO. It means SEPARATED or DETACHED.
To play STACCATO, *release* the key instantly.

STACCATO is indicated by a DOT over ♩ or under ♩ the note.

Ping-Pong

Brightly

I play ping-pong with my Dad and some-times let him win! (Oops!)

When he hits the ball too hard I fetch it back a - gain! (Out!)

INCOMPLETE MEASURE

Some pieces begin with an INCOMPLETE MEASURE. The first measure in this piece has only **1** count. The 3 missing counts are found in the last measure. When you repeat the whole piece, you will have one whole measure of 4 counts when you play the last measure plus the first measure.

Grandpa's Clock

Moderately fast

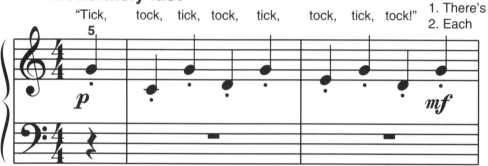

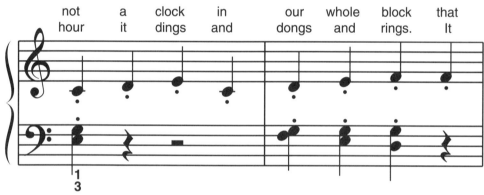

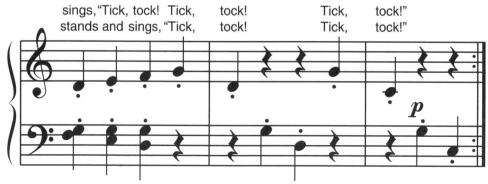

When the Saints Go Marching In

March time

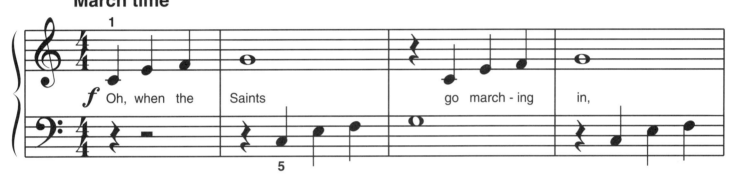

TIE: hold for combined value of both notes.

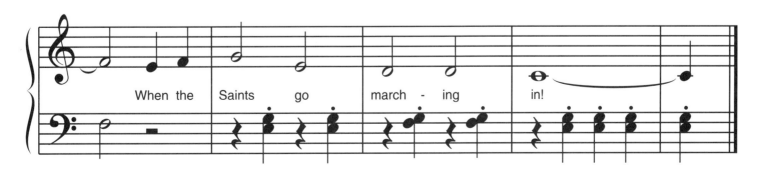

G Position Review

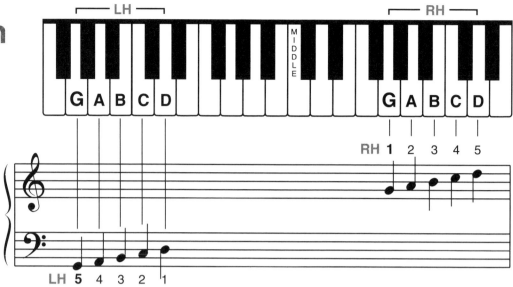

Play and say the note names.

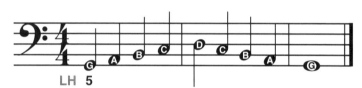 

G's in the "BAG"

Moderately fast

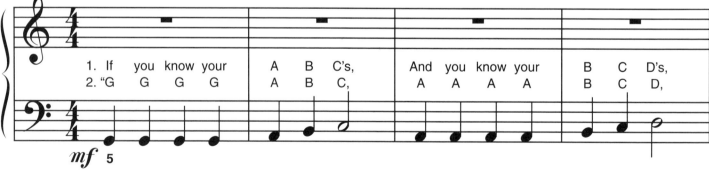

1. If you know your A B C's, And you know your B C D's,
2. "G G G G A A A A B C D,

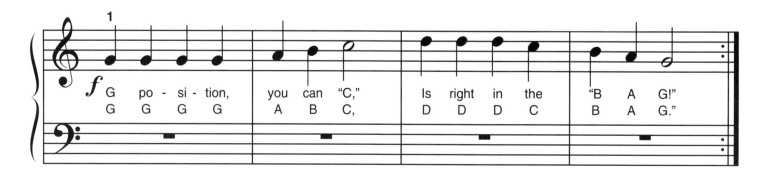

f G po-si-tion, you can "C," Is right in the "B A G!"
G G G G A B C, D D D C B A G."

REVIEW: Dynamic Signs

CRESCENDO (gradually louder) **DIMINUENDO** (gradually softer)

Join the Fun

14

This is an **ACCENT SIGN.**

> When there is an ACCENT SIGN over or under a note, play that note LOUDER.

Oom-Pa-pa!

Moderately fast

mf
1. Pa - pa bought a horn for me to play in the sym - pho - ny.
2. When the bass be - gins to boom, Ev - 'ry pa - pa needs an oom!

"With this horn," he told my ma, "He'll play oom for his pa - pa!"
Like a babe needs its ma - ma, Ev - 'ry oom needs its pa - pa!

f Oom - pa, oom - pa, oom - pa - pa! Oom - pa, oom - pa oom - pa - pa!

Oom - pa, oom - pa, oom - pa - pa! "He'll play oom for his pa - pa!"
Ev - 'ry oom needs its pa - pa!

Suggestion: After playing the entire piece twice, repeat the last two lines again, playing the LH one octave lower!

Reviewing the FLAT SIGN

♭ The FLAT SIGN before a note means
play the next key to the LEFT,
whether BLACK or WHITE.

When a FLAT SIGN appears before a note,
it applies to that note for the rest of the measure.

The Clown

Moderately fast

See the fun - ny, fun - ny clown. *mf*
He climbs up and he falls down!

You will nev - er see him frown! *mf*
He's a fun - ny clown.

Fine

f Al - ways be a glad clown! Al - ways steal the show!

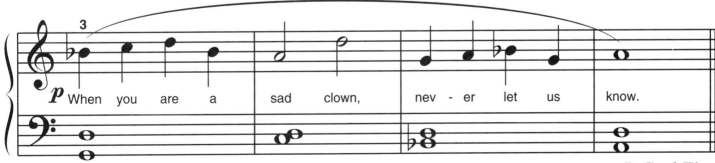

p When you are a sad clown, nev - er let us know.

D.C. al Fine

D.C. al Fine (Da Capo al Fine) means *repeat from the beginning and play to the end (Fine).*

Reading in Middle C Position

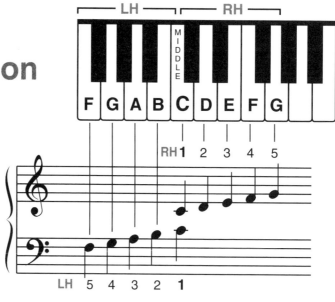

Both thumbs on MIDDLE C!

Play and say the note names.

NEW NOTES

Thumbs on C!

Moderately slow

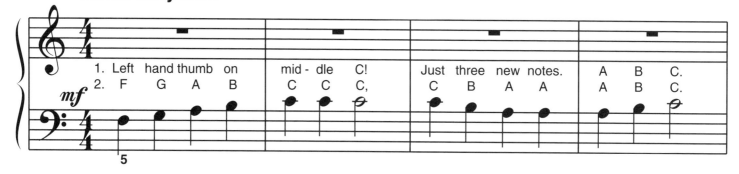

1. Left hand thumb on mid - dle C! Just three new notes. A B C.
2. F G A B C C C, C B A A A B C.

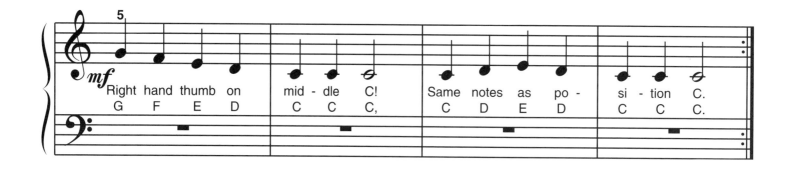

Right hand thumb on mid - dle C! Same notes as po - si - tion C.
G F E D C C C, C D E D C C C.

Tempo Marks

TEMPO is an Italian word. It means "RATE OF SPEED."

Words indicating how fast or slow to play
are called **TEMPO MARKS.**

Here are some of the most important tempo marks:

ALLEGRO = Quickly, happily.
MODERATO = Moderately.
ANDANTE = Moving along. The word actually means "walking."
ADAGIO = Slowly.

Waltz Time

MIDDLE C POSITION

Bring out the LH melody.

Suggestion: Repeat with both hands one octave higher.

Good King Wenceslas

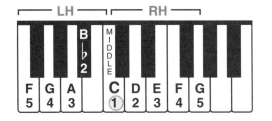

Allegro moderato (moderately fast)

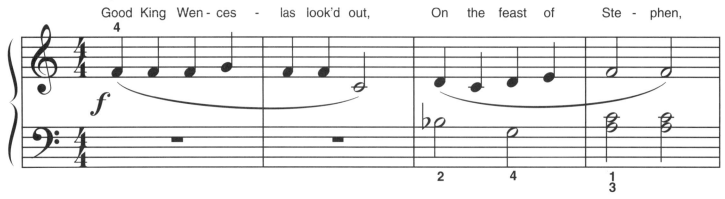

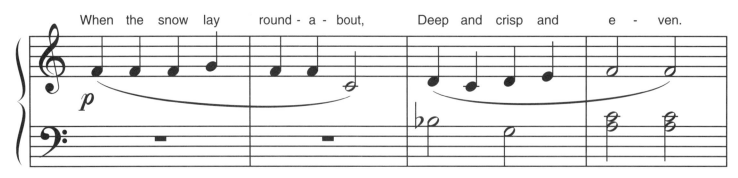

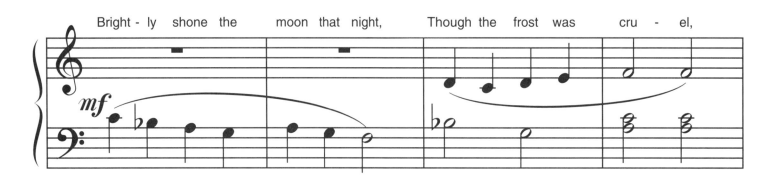

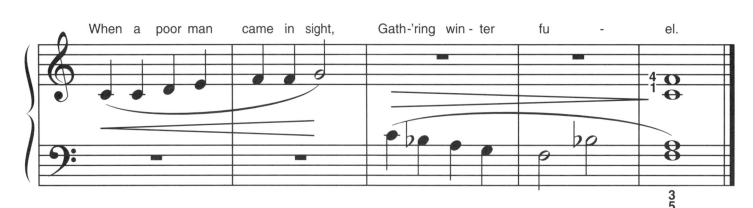

The Rainbow

 This sign is called a **FERMATA.**

Hold the note under the FERMATA longer than its value.

Roy G. Biv*

Andante (moving along)

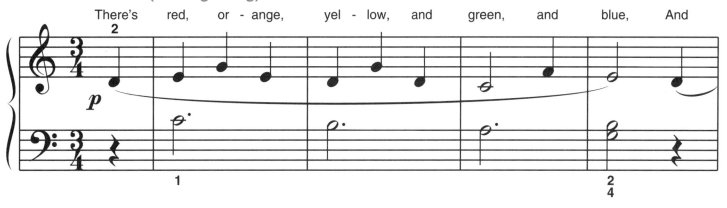

There's red, or-ange, yel-low, and green, and blue, And

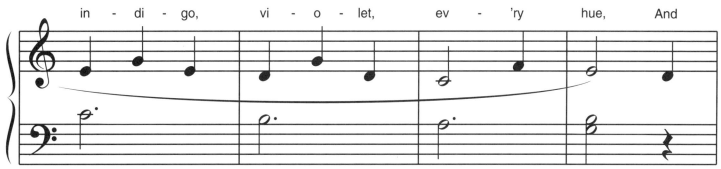

in-di-go, vi-o-let, ev-'ry hue, And

Adagio (slowly)

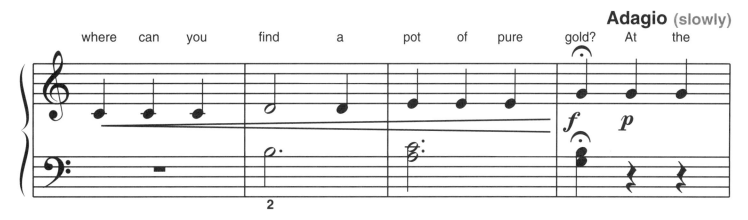

where can you find a pot of pure gold? At the

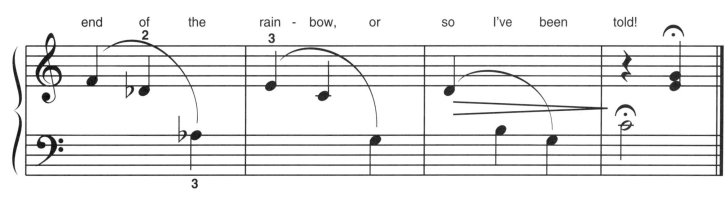

end of the rain-bow, or so I've been told!

*Remember the name "Roy G. Biv" and you will always know the colors of the rainbow in the order in which they appear.

Good Morning to You!

Allegro (quickly, happily)

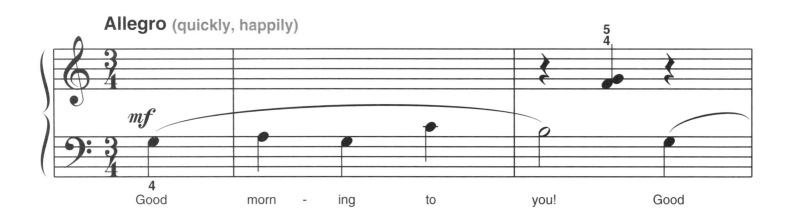

Good   morn - ing   to   you!   Good

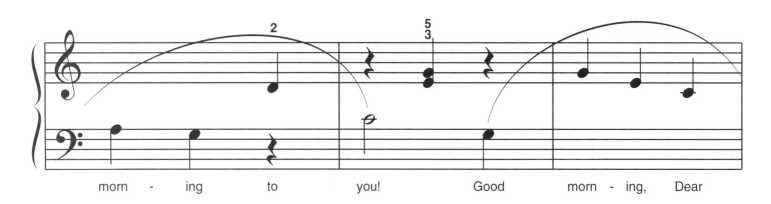

morn - ing   to   you!   Good   morn - ing,   Dear

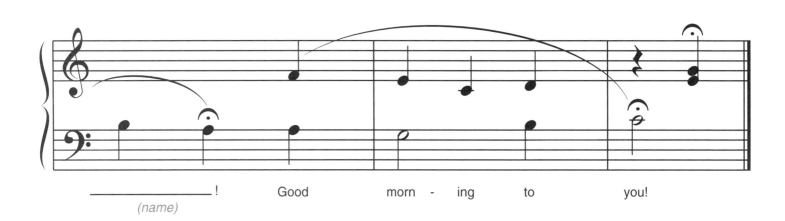

_____! Good   morn - ing   to   you!
(name)

Eighth Notes

Two eighth notes are played in the time of **one quarter note**.

Eighth notes are usually played in **pairs.**

COUNT: "one-and"
or: "two-8ths"

When a piece contains eighth notes,

count: **"one-and"** or **"quar-ter"** for each quarter note;
count: **"one-and"** or **"two-8ths"** for each pair of eighth notes.

Clap (or tap) these notes, counting aloud.

Happy Birthday to You!

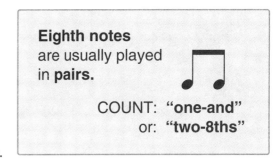

HAPPY BIRTHDAY is exactly the same as *GOOD MORNING TO YOU,* except for the EIGHTH NOTES!

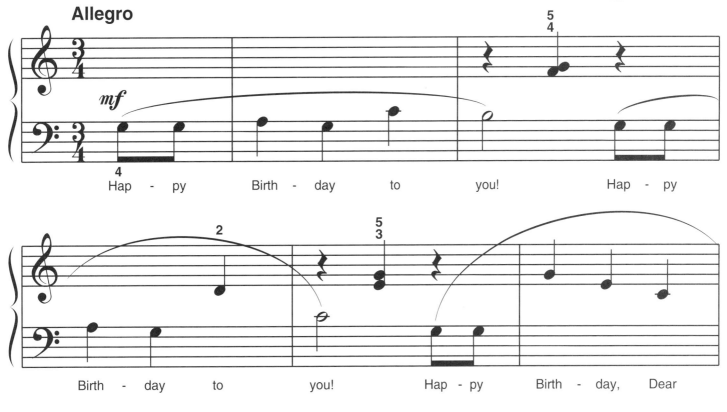

Allegro

mf

Hap - py   Birth - day   to   you!   Hap - py

Birth - day   to   you!   Hap - py   Birth - day,   Dear

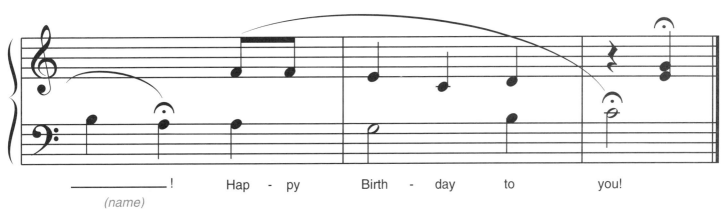

_____!   Hap - py   Birth - day   to   you!

(name)

A NEW TIME SIGNATURE

2/4 means **2** beats to each measure.

a **quarter note** gets one beat.

Clap (or tap) the following rhythm.
Clap **ONCE** for each note, counting aloud.

Yankee Doodle

A **WHOLE REST** is used to indicate a
whole measure of silence in **2/4** time.

Allegro moderato

Yan - kee Doo - dle   went to town,   Rid - ing on a   po - ny, He

stuck a feath - er   in his hat and   called it mac - a - ro - ni!

DUET PART: (Student plays 1 octave higher.)

> *ritardando* means GRADUALLY SLOWING THE TEMPO.
> It is often abbreviated *ritard.* or *rit.*
> The words *a tempo* mean RESUME THE ORIGINAL TEMPO.

The Windmill

Andante

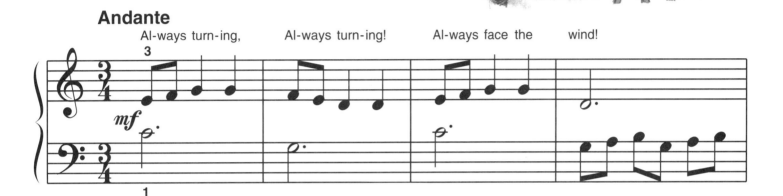

Al-ways turn-ing, Al-ways turn-ing! Al-ways face the wind!

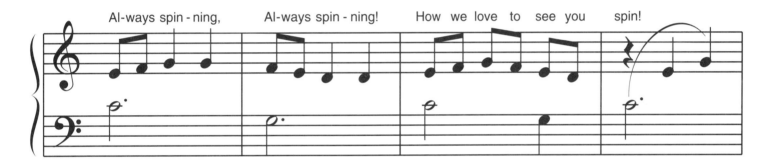

Al-ways spin - ning, Al-ways spin - ning! How we love to see you spin!

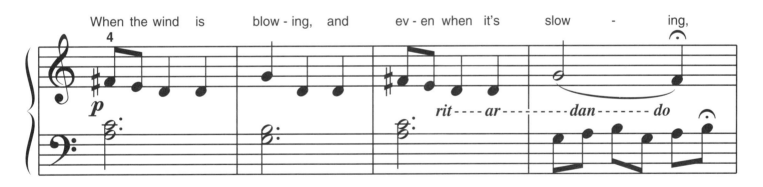

When the wind is blow - ing, and ev - en when it's slow - ing,

rit - - - - ar - - - - - - - dan - - - - - do

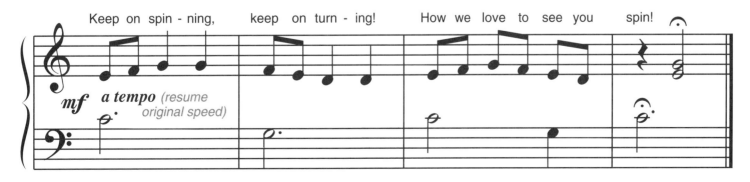

Keep on spin - ning, keep on turn - ing! How we love to see you spin!

mf *a tempo* *(resume original speed)*

Suggestion: For recital performance, repeat *THE WINDMILL,* playing both hands one octave higher; then play the last line AGAIN, very slowly and softly.

24

Indians

G POSITION

Moderato

1. Cher-o-kee, Chick-a-saw, Chat-ta-wa, Chip-pe-wa, too,
2. Kick-a-poo, Ki-o-wa, Ot-ta-wa, I-o-wa, Sioux.*

mf

f In-di-an na-tions, here be-fore The great Chris-to-pher Co-lum-bus came!
And there were man-y, man-y more, See how man-y na-tions you can name!

mf Paw-nee, A-ra-pa-ho, Shaw-nee and Na-va-ho, too.

p   *rit - - - - - - - - - ar - - - - - - - - - - dan - - - - - - - - - - do*

*Note: *Sioux* is pronounced "Soo." It rhymes with "too."

The double dots inside the double bars indicate
that everything between the double bars must be REPEATED.

G Position with LH an Octave Higher

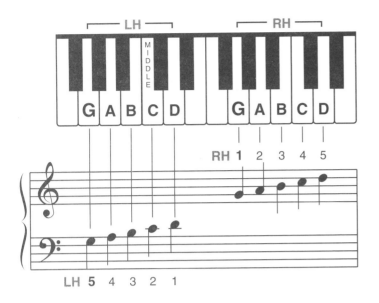

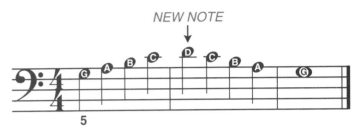

In this NEW G POSITION, the LEFT HAND plays ONE OCTAVE HIGHER than before. The RIGHT HAND remains in the same position.

There is only ONE new LH note to learn.

NEW NOTE

New Position G

Moderato

1. G, G, Gee what fun, play - ing up to D!
2. G G G A B, B A B C D,

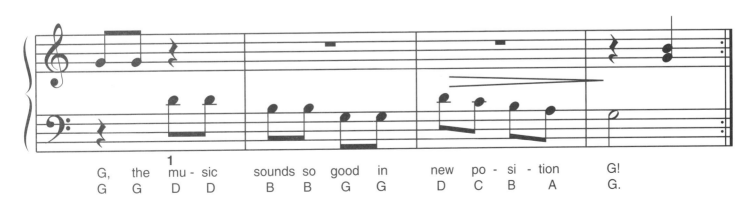

G, the mu - sic sounds so good in new po - si - tion G!
G G D D B B G G D C B A G.

The Damper Pedal

The RIGHT PEDAL is called the **DAMPER PEDAL**.

When you hold the damper pedal down, any tone you sound continues after you release the key.

The RIGHT FOOT is used on the damper pedal.
Always keep your heel on the floor;
use your ankle like a hinge.

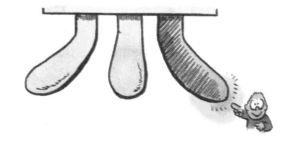

This sign shows when the damper pedal is to be used: ⌐‾‾‾‾‾‾‾‾‾‾‾¬

The sign means: **PEDAL DOWN**

HOLD PEDAL **PEDAL UP**

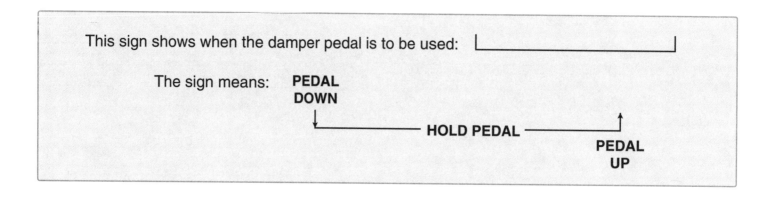

Pedal Play

This easy PEDAL STUDY will show you how the damper pedal causes the tones to continue to sound, EVEN AFTER YOUR HANDS HAVE RELEASED THE KEYS.

Press the pedal down as you play each group of notes. Hold it down through the rests.

Play **VERY SLOWLY** and **LISTEN.**

Adagio

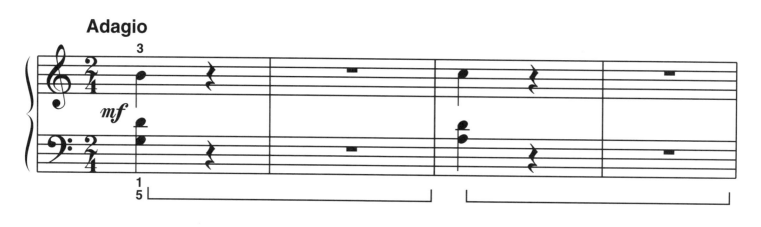

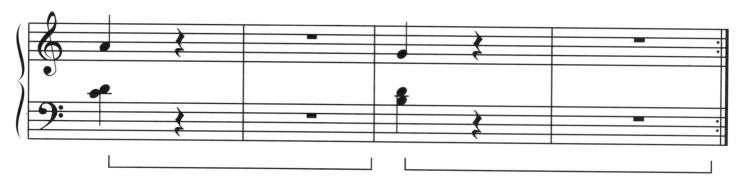

Harp Song

Moderately slow

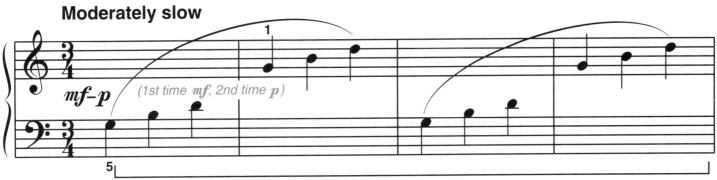

mf–p   (1st time *mf*, 2nd time *p*)

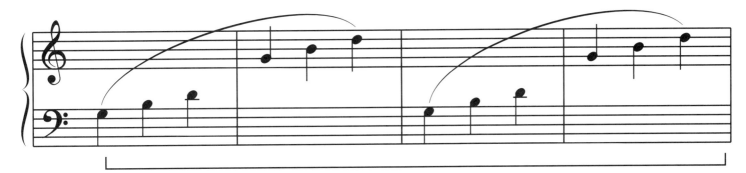

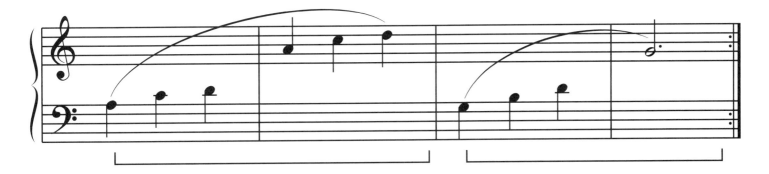

VERY IMPORTANT!

Also play *HARP SONG* in the following ways:

1. Play the 3rd and 4th measures of each line one octave higher than written.
2. Play the 1st and 2nd measures of each line one octave lower than written.
3. Any combination of the above two ways.

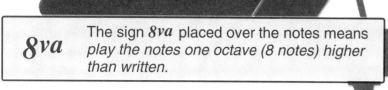

8va   The sign *8va* placed over the notes means *play the notes one octave (8 notes) higher than written.*

Concert Time

Allegro moderato

Both hands *8va**

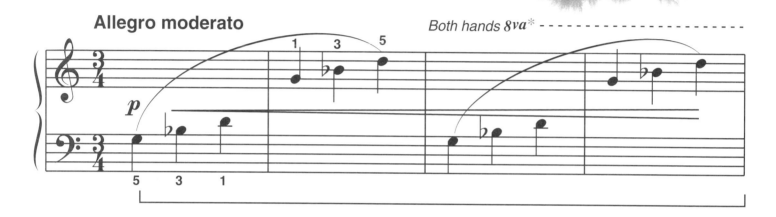

Both hands *8va*

Fine

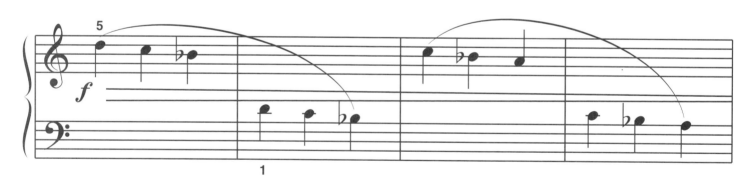

8va applies only to the STAFF below it unless "both hands" is added.

D.C. al Fine

Music Box Rock

Allegro

Play both hands 8va throughout.

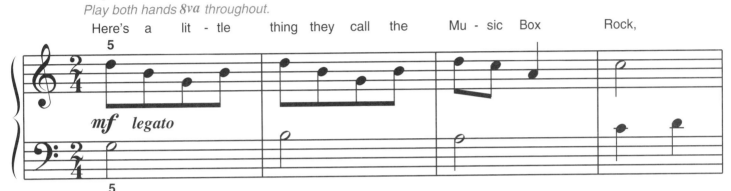

Here's a lit - tle thing they call the Mu - sic Box Rock,

mf legato

Mu - sic Box Rock, Mu - sic Box Rock!

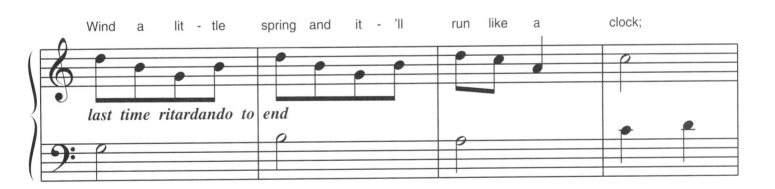

Wind a lit - tle spring and it - 'll run like a clock;

last time ritardando to end

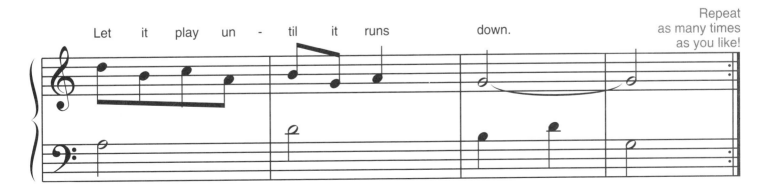

Let it play un - til it runs down.

Repeat
as many times
as you like!

A Cowboy's Song

Lazily

5 1 4 1 3

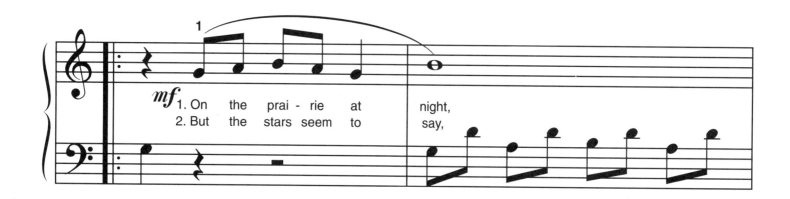

mf 1. On   the   prai - rie   at   night,
    2. But   the   stars   seem   to   say,

A special WESTERN EFFECT may be produced by playing the pairs of eighth notes a bit unevenly, in a "lilting" style:

long   short   long   short, *etc.*

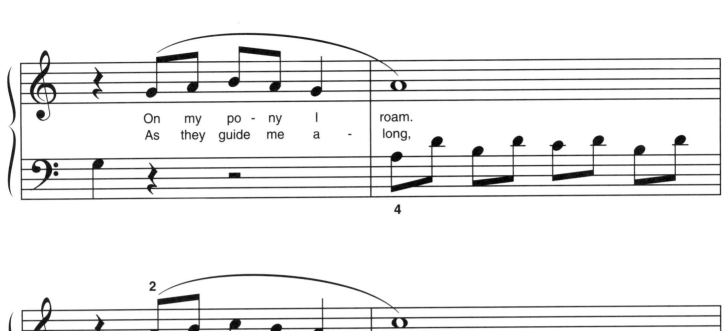

On my po - ny I roam.
As they guide me a - long,

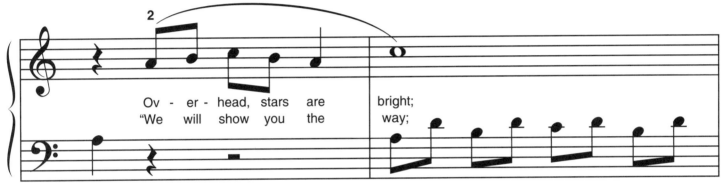

Ov - er - head, stars are bright;
"We will show you the way;

I'm a long way from home!
We won't let you go wrong!"

rit - - - - - - - - ar - - - - - - - dan - - - - - - - do - - - - - - - - - - - - - - -   *p*

Suggestion: Play *A COWBOY'S SONG* also with LH *8va* **lower,** in the old G position.

This is an **EIGHTH REST:**

It means REST FOR THE VALUE OF AN EIGHTH NOTE.

When eighth notes appear singly, they look like this:

Single eighth notes are often used with eighth rests.

COUNT: "one - and"
OR: "two - 8ths"

Clap (or tap) the following rhythm:

The Magic Man

Mysteriously

1. Who can pull a rab-bit out of
2. Who can van-ish an-y-thing and

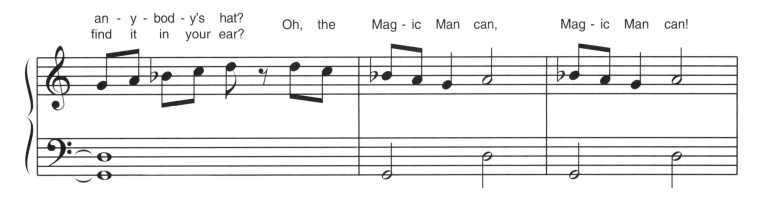

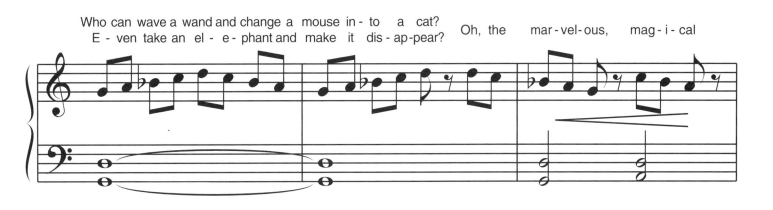

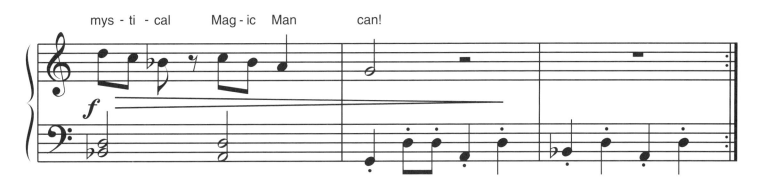

MIDDLE D POSITION

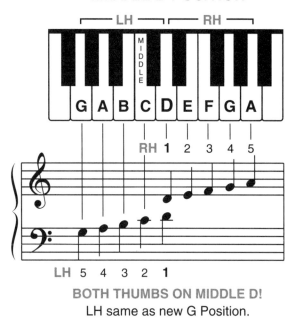

BOTH THUMBS ON MIDDLE D!
LH same as new G Position.

The Greatest Show on Earth!

March tempo

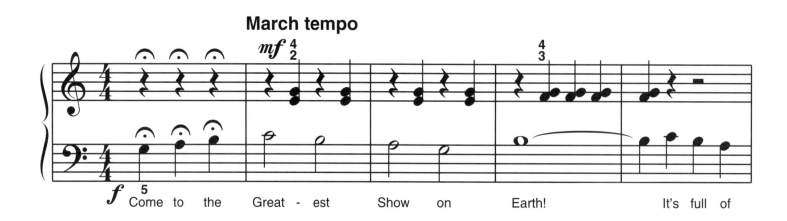

f Come to the Great - est Show on Earth! It's full of

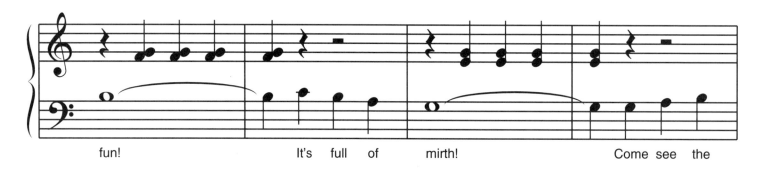

fun! It's full of mirth! Come see the

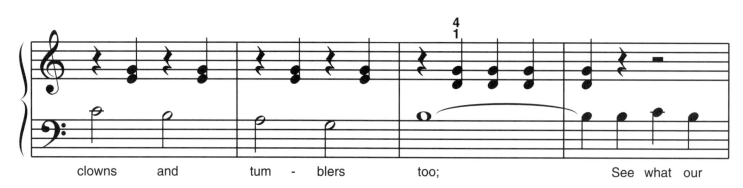

clowns and tum - blers too; See what our

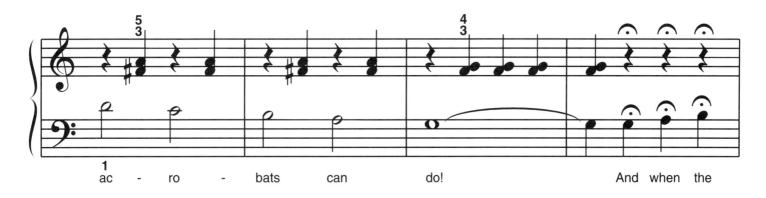

ac - ro - bats can do! And when the

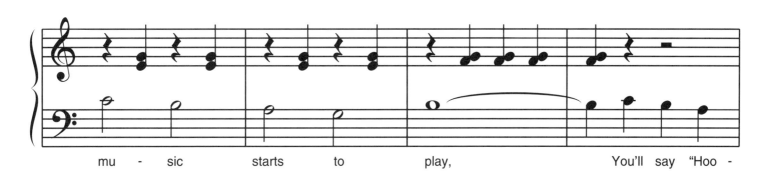

mu - sic starts to play, You'll say "Hoo -

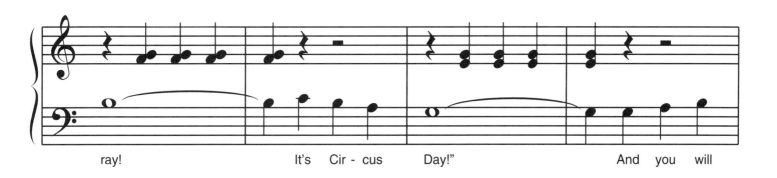

ray! It's Cir - cus Day!" And you will

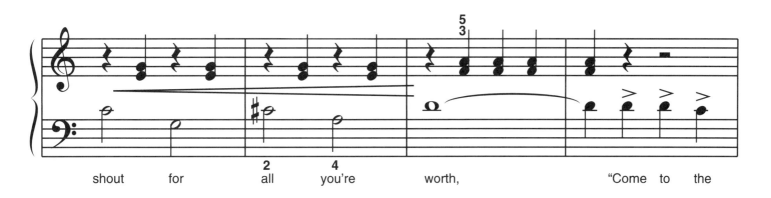

shout for all you're worth, "Come to the

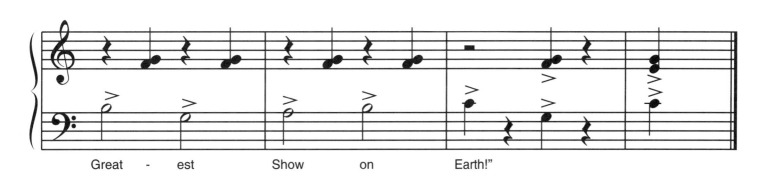

Great - est Show on Earth!"

Measuring Half Steps

A **HALF STEP** is the distance from any key to the very next key up or down, black or white, with **NO KEY BETWEEN.**

The SHARP sign ♯ raises a note a half step.

The FLAT sign ♭ lowers a note a half step.

Each black key may be named 2 ways, as shown here:

The NATURAL sign ♮ is used to **CANCEL** a sharp or flat.

A note after a natural is **ALWAYS** a **WHITE KEY!**

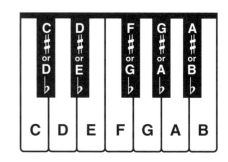

Middle D "Half Step" Position

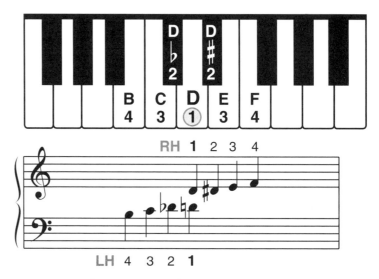

BOTH THUMBS ON MIDDLE D!

Play & count:

The Whirlwind

MIDDLE D "HALF STEP" POSITION

This piece consists entirely of half steps,
except for the last two measures.

Allegro moderato

1. Whist - ling, whirl - ing,   twist - ing, turn - ing,   Soar - ing, swirl - ing,   chas - ing, churn - ing,
2. Whip - ping, whisk - ing,   curv - ing, curl - ing,   Flit - ting, frisk - ing,   hum - ming, hurl - ing,

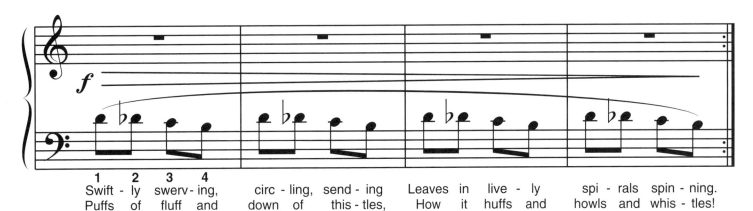

Swift - ly swerv - ing,   circ - ling, send - ing   Leaves in live - ly   spi - rals spin - ning.
Puffs of fluff and   down of this - tles,   How it huffs and   howls and whis - tles!

Diz - zi - ly   it   winds and chas - es   Ev - 'ry - thing   it   finds and rac - es

Whirl - ing, twirl - ing,   swirl - ing out of   sight!

Measuring Whole Steps

A **WHOLE STEP** is equal to 2 HALF STEPS
with **ONE KEY BETWEEN.**

Middle D "Whole Step" Position

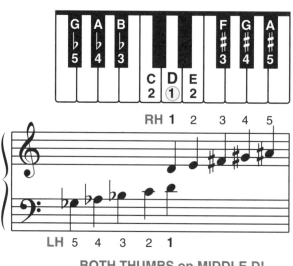

BOTH THUMBS on MIDDLE D!

When a SHARP or FLAT appears before a note, it applies to that note each time
it is used in the rest of the measure, unless it is cancelled by a natural.

A SHARP or FLAT continues when a note is tied to the following measure.
It is not necessary to re-write the sharp or flat before the second of the two tied notes.

Play & count:

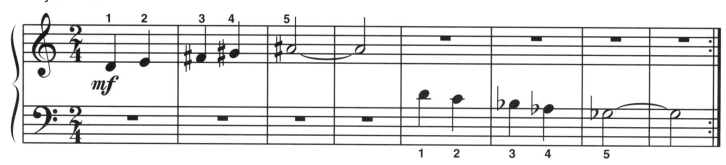

The Planets

MIDDLE D "WHOLE STEP" POSITION

Andante

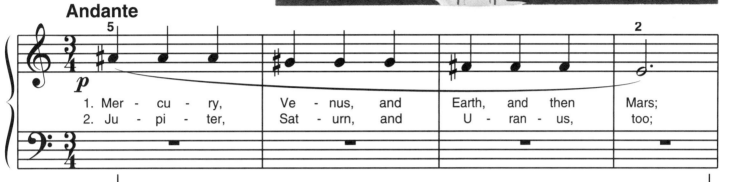

1. Mer - cu - ry, Ve - nus, and Earth, and then Mars;
2. Ju - pi - ter, Sat - urn, and U - ran - us, too;

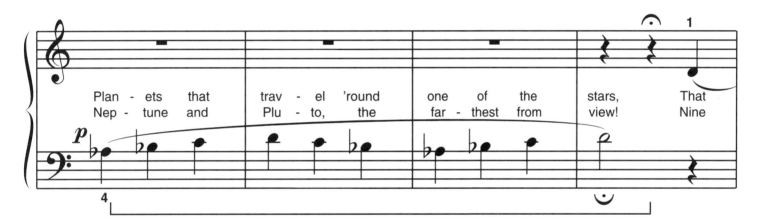

Plan - ets that trav - el 'round one of the stars, view! That
Nep - tune and Plu - to, round the far - thest from Nine

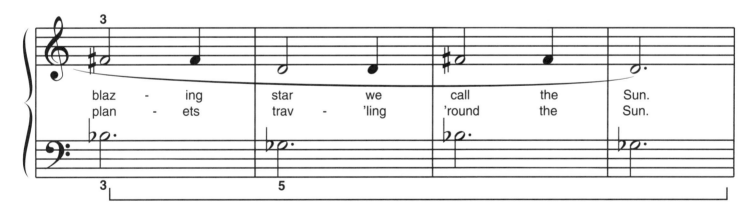

blaz - ing star we call the Sun.
plan - ets trav - 'ling 'round the Sun.

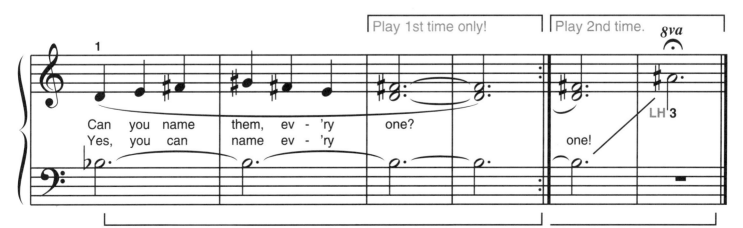

Play 1st time only! Play 2nd time.

Can you name them, ev - 'ry one? one!
Yes, you can name ev - 'ry

Tetrachords

A TETRACHORD is a series of FOUR NOTES having a pattern of

WHOLE STEP, WHOLE STEP, HALF STEP

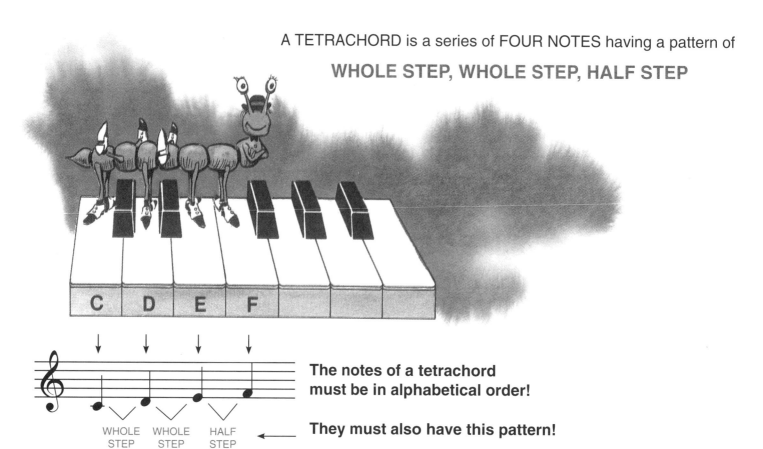

The notes of a tetrachord must be in alphabetical order!

They must also have this pattern!

Play the following tetrachords.

LH tetrachords are fingered **5 4 3 2.**

C TETRACHORDS:

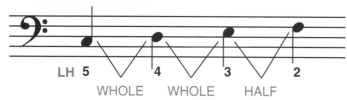

RH tetrachords are fingered **2 3 4 5.**

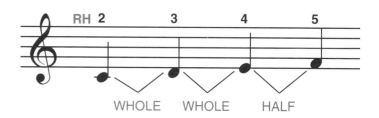

G TETRACHORDS:

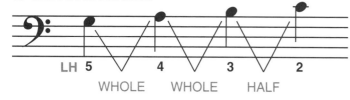

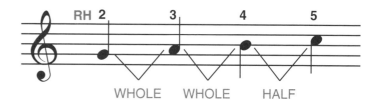

D TETRACHORDS:

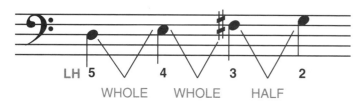

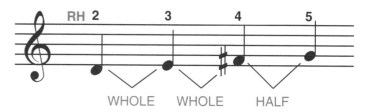

The Major Scale

The MAJOR SCALE is made of **TWO TETRACHORDS** *joined* by a **WHOLE STEP.**

THE C MAJOR SCALE

There is **NO ♯** or ♭ in the *C MAJOR SCALE.*

Each scale begins and ends on a note of the same name as the scale, called the **KEY-NOTE.**

C Major Scale Piece

Both 5's play the **KEY-NOTE, C!**

1. Play whole, whole, half.   Play whole, whole, half.   Then come down the   ver - y same way!
2. Watch the half steps!   Watch the half steps!   Tet - ra - chords are   eas - y   to   play!

THE G MAJOR SCALE

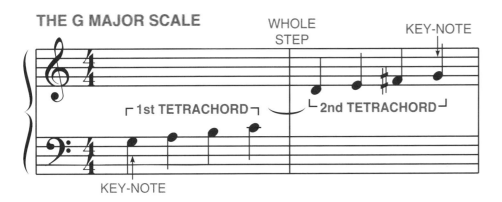

There is **ONE ♯** *(F♯)* in the *G MAJOR SCALE.*

G Major Scale Piece

Both 5's play the **KEY-NOTE, G!**

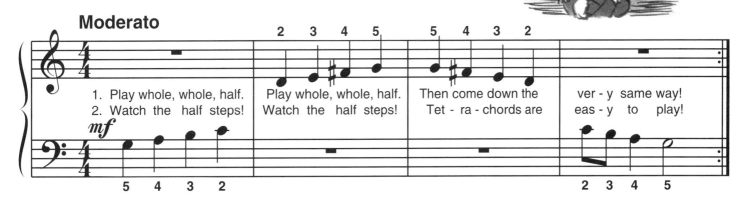

Moderato

1. Play whole, whole, half.   Play whole, whole, half.   Then come down the   ver - y same way!
2. Watch the half steps!   Watch the half steps!   Tet - ra - chords are   eas - y   to   play!

The Key of G Major

A piece based on the G major scale is in the **KEY OF G MAJOR.**
Since F is sharp in the G scale, every F is sharp.

Instead of placing a sharp before every F, the sharp is indicated
at the beginning in the KEY SIGNATURE.

Carol in G Major

KEY OF G MAJOR
Key Signature: one sharp (F♯)
Play all "F's" sharp throughout.

HAND POSITION: RH plays the upper tetrachord,
LH plays the lower tetrachord.

Moderato

mf While   by   my   sheep   I   watched   at   night,

Glad   tid - ings   brought   the   an - gel   bright.

The Same Carol in C Major

KEY OF C MAJOR
Key Signature: no ♯, no ♭

HAND POSITION: RH plays the upper tetrachord,
LH plays the lower tetrachord.

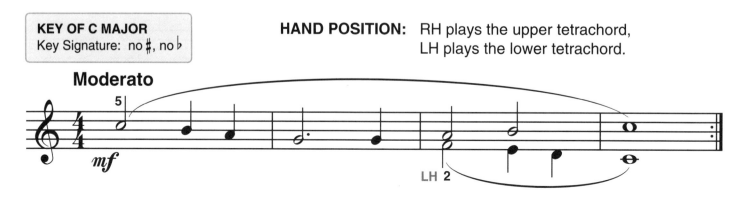

Moderato

mf

LH 2

A Piece with 2 LH Positions

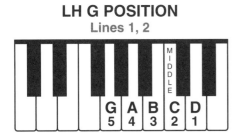 **LH G POSITION**
Lines 1, 2

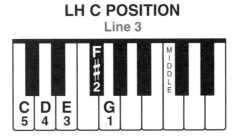 **LH C POSITION**
Line 3

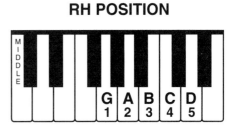 **RH POSITION**

From the KEY SIGNATURE you will see that this piece is
in the KEY OF G MAJOR—all F's must be SHARPED.
Watch for the F's in the LH part of the last line!

French Lullaby

last time ritard.

(After repeating,
move LH to
C POSITION)

Fine

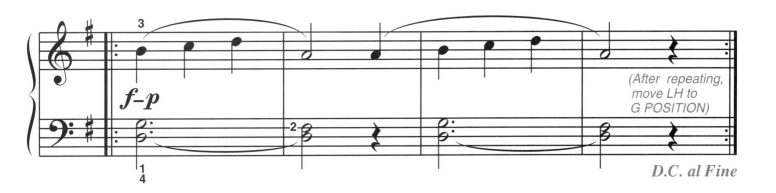

(After repeating,
move LH to
G POSITION)

D.C. al Fine

A Piece with 2 RH Positions

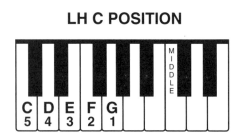

LH C POSITION

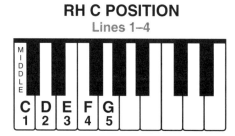

RH C POSITION
Lines 1–4

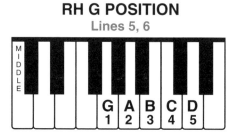

RH G POSITION
Lines 5, 6

The piece begins in the KEY OF C MAJOR, changes to the KEY OF G MAJOR, then returns to C MAJOR. Be sure to make all the F's sharp in the 5th and 6th lines.

Sonatina

KEY OF C MAJOR
Key Signature: no ♯, no ♭

Allegro moderato

A *SONATINA* is a short instrumental selection. It may have one, two, or three movements.   If the first or only movement begins in the key of C major, the second part of the movement is usually in the key of G major. The movement returns to the original key at the end.

2nd time ritardando (Move RH to G POSITION)

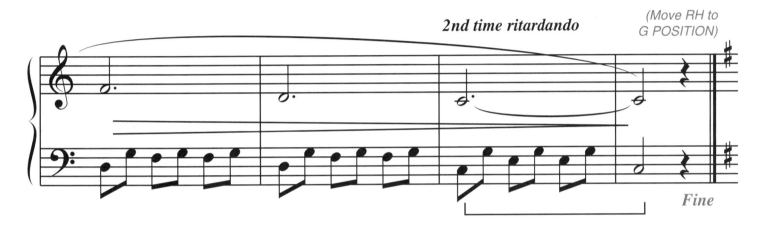

Fine

KEY OF G MAJOR
Key Signature: 1 sharp (F♯)

(Move RH to C POSITION)

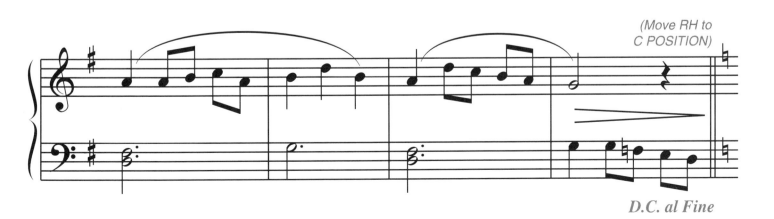

D.C. al Fine

When Our Band Goes Marching By!

This piece is in the **KEY OF C MAJOR.** Although there are no sharps or flats in the key signature, some sharps occur during the piece. Sharps or flats not in the key signature are called **ACCIDENTALS.**

C POSITION

Review of Musical Terms

Accent (>) . . . . placed over or under a note that gets special emphasis.
Play the note louder.

Accidental . . . . a sharp or flat not given in the key signature.

Adagio . . . . slowly.

Allegro . . . . quickly, happily.

Andante . . . . moving along (at walking speed).

A tempo . . . . resume original speed.

Crescendo (————————) . . . . gradually louder.

Da Capo al Fine (D.C. al Fine) . . . . . . repeat from the beginning and play to the Fine (end).

Diminuendo (————————) . . . . . gradually softer.

Dynamic signs . . . . signs showing how loud or soft to play.

Fermata (⌒) . . . . indicates that a note should be held longer than its true value.

Fine . . . . the end.

First ending (1. ⌐——¬) . . . . the measures under the bracket are played the 1st time only.

Flat sign (♭) . . . . lowers a note one half step. Play the next key to the left.

Forte (f) . . . . loud.

Half step . . . . the distance from one key to the very next one, with no key
between.

Harmonic interval . . . . the interval between two tones sounded together.

Incomplete measure . . . . a measure at the beginning of a piece with fewer counts than
shown in the time signatures. The missing counts are found in
the last measure.

Interval . . . . the difference in pitch (highness or lowness) between two tones.

Key signature . . . . the number of sharps or flats in any key—written at the beginning
of each line.

Legato . . . . smoothly connected. Usually indicated by a slur over or under the notes.

Major scale . . . . a series of 8 notes made of two tetrachords joined by a whole step.

Melodic interval . . . . the interval between two tones sounded separately.

Mezzo forte (mf) . . . . moderately loud.

Moderato . . . . moderately.

Natural sign (♮) . . . . cancels a sharp or flat.

Octave sign (8va) . . . . when placed OVER notes, means play them one octave higher
than written.

Pedal mark (⌐————⌐) . . . . press the damper pedal, hold it, and release it.

Piano (p) . . . . soft.

Repeat signs 〓〓〓〓‖ . . . repeat from the beginning.

‖〓〓〓〓‖ . . . repeat the measures between the double bars.

Ritardando (abbreviated ritard. . . . . . gradually slowing.
or rit.)

Second ending (2. ⌐——¬) . . . . the measures under the bracket are played the 2nd time only.

Sharp sign (♯) . . . . raises a note one half step. Play the next key to the right.

Staccato . . . . separated or detached. Usually indicated by a dot over or under
the note.

Tempo . . . . rate of speed.

Tetrachord . . . . four notes in alphabetical order, having the pattern of
WHOLE STEP, WHOLE STEP, HALF STEP.

Time signatures ($\frac{2}{4}$, $\frac{3}{4}$, $\frac{4}{4}$) . . . . numbers found at the beginning of a piece or section of a piece.
The top number shows the number of beats in each measure.
The bottom number shows the kind of note that gets one beat.

Whole step . . . . two half steps. The distance between two keys with one key between.

Certificate of Promotion

This is to certify that

_____

has successfully completed Level 1B
of the LESSON BOOK and is hereby promoted
to Level 2 of Alfred's Basic Piano Library.

_____
Date

_____
Teacher